Languages of the World

A Multi-Lingual Introduction to Letters from Around the Globe

Appropriate for Children Ages 2-4

Volume 1

Brian P. Sheets

Languages of the World

A Multi-Lingual Introduction to Letters from Around the Globe

Published by:

Priati Publications (a division of Pria Technologies Inc.)

14845 SW Murray Scholls Dr.

Ste 110 PMB 130

Beaverton, Oregon 97007 USA

www.priatipub.com

info@priatipub.com

ISBN 978-0-9971108-0-7

Copyright © 2016 Brian P. Sheets

Printed in the United States of America

All rights reserved. No part of this book may be reproduced or transmitted in any form or by any means, electronic or mechanical, including photocopying, recording, or by any information storage and retrieval system without written permission from the author, except for the inclusion of brief quotations in a review. It is illegal to copy this book, post it to a website, or distribute it by any other means without permission from the publisher.

Limits of Liability and Disclaimer of Warranty

This book is strictly for informational, educational, and entertainment purposes. The author and/or publisher do not guarantee that anyone following these techniques, suggestions, tips, ideas, or strategies will become successful. The author and publisher shall have neither liability nor responsibility to anyone with respect to any loss or damage caused, or alleged to be caused, directly or indirectly, by the information contained in this book or the reader's misuse of this material.

Like this book?

If you like this author's work, your favorable review would be greatly appreciated.

Other publications by this author can be found at:

http://www.priatipub.com

Languages of the World – A Multi-Lingual Introduction to Letters from Around the Globe – Volume 1 **[2017 eLit Gold Award for Education / Academics / Teaching]**

Languages of the World – A Multi-Lingual Introduction to Numbers from Around the Globe – Volume 2 **[2017 eLit Gold Award for Children's Books (7 & Under)]**

Languages of the World – A Multi-Lingual Introduction to Words from Around the Globe – Volume 3 **[2018 eLit Gold Award for Education / Academics / Teaching]**

The Rest Areas of Your Life   (Kindle eBook)

A Practical Approach to Parenting   (Kindle eBook)

Two Images of God – Quest – Book 1   (Suspense Novel) **[2018 Reader's Favorite Finalist]**

Two Images of God – Discontent – Book 2   (Suspense Novel)

Two Images of God – Conflict – Book 3   (Suspense Novel)

Contents

Introduction 6
Languages 8
The Letter A 10
The Letter B 11
The Letter C 12
The Letter D 13
The Letter E 14
The Letter F 15
The Letter G 16
The Letter H 17
The Letter I 18
The Letter J 19
The Letter K 20
The Letter L 21
The Letter M 22
The Letter N 23
The Letter O 24
The Letter P 25
The Letter Q 26
The Letter R 27
The Letter S 28
The Letter T 29
The Letter U 30
The Letter V 31
The Letter W 32
The Letter X 33
The Letter Y 34
The Letter Z 35
Author's Note 36
Publisher's Note 37
Other Books by Author 38

Endnotes..39

Introduction

I would like to personally thank you for allowing me the opportunity to share this instructional material with you and your family. As your child begins their life journey into the world of literature, much of their future success will be determined by the level of appreciation they attain in the world of words.

Many children have learned their "A – B – C's" through the rote memorization of simple songs. However, studies have shown that learning the sequence of letters does little for teaching a child how to form words. Rather, it is through the correct pronunciation of each letter or combination of letters, combined with how the letter(s) sounds in word usage, which promotes growth in vocabulary and reading.

This book includes phonetic aids in teaching a child how to correctly pronounce each letter in English. If the letter is a vowel, it includes examples of both "long" and "short" vowel sounds (for example, Ā and ă). This is reinforced by showing sample words that reflect the correct pronunciation of each letter and those with long & short vowels. Not included are special circumstances such as two vowels appearing together [i.e. "(i) before (e) except after (c)"]. It was felt that concepts such as these are more appropriately taught to children more mature than the target age of this book.

Example Page Information

Each page is arranged in a common format similar to what appears below. If a vowel, both the long vowel and short vowel sounds are shown. For letters which are not vowels, no "Symbol" line will appear.

Symbol	Ō, ŏ	If a vowel, both the long and short vowels are shown.
Phonetics	O, Ahh	The letter is shown in a phonetic pronunciation (for long and short vowels)
English	Open, Top	Sample words that reflect the proper sound of the letter (for long and short vowels)
French	Ouvert, Haut	French equivalent word.
German	Geöffnet, oberste	German equivalent word.

Not all foreign languages have a direct equivalent translation for the English word that appears. In such cases, a word has been selected that is similar to, or conveys the essence of, the English word shown.

In summary, this book seeks to educate the reader in basic letter concepts and an appreciation for how letters form translatable words in cultures different than their own.

Best of luck in your journey!

Sincerely,

Brian P. Sheets

Author

Languages

It is reported that there are more than 6,000 spoken languages in the world. Since we have become a global society, future generations that develop an appreciation for other languages will find more economic and personal satisfaction in life for having taken the time to develop this skill.

The eleven languages selected for this book series represent those spoken by the greatest number of people around the globe or those languages for which there is a higher social interest via travel. Using English as the base language for this book, phonetic pronunciations have also been included to aid in properly sounding out each English letter. The languages selected include:

English

French

German

Italian

Japanese (Romaji)

Korean (RRK)

Indonesian

Mandarin (Hanyu Pinyin)

Portuguese

Russian

Spanish

Each page will display these eleven different languages. For Japanese, Korean, and Mandarin, their Romanized equivalent word is shown in Romaji (Japanese), RRK[1] (Korean), and Hanyu Pinyin (Mandarin) as opposed to using their native language written calligraphy (Japanese Kanji, Korean Hanja, and Mandarin Hanzi).

While Arabic is a widely used language, there is no commonly used or agreed upon transliteration. While different approaches and methods for the Romanization of Arabic exist, they vary in the way that they address the inherent problems of rendering written and spoken Arabic in the Latin script.[2] Accordingly, it has not been included in this book.

While this book was written for people for whom English is their native tongue, the translations included herein can be used three ways. First, English-speaking children can use this book as a primer to begin learning how letters appear and are pronounced in English. Second, children may use this book to see how English letters and words appear in different cultures, thus using this book as a springboard to learn another language. Finally, for those whose native tongue is not English (such as ESL programs), this book can be used to learn the basics of how letters appear and sound in the English language. Accordingly, this book can be used by nearly any culture to introduce a child to different languages used for common terms.

As parents, you can take pride in knowing that you are taking a positive first step in guiding the success of your child through developing an appreciation for what other cultures have to offer in a world made smaller by technology, travel, and words.

Enjoy the journey!

The Letter A

Ā, ă

As a vowel, the letter 'A' can appear and sound differently. It can have a long 'A' (Ā) sound as in the word "cake", or a short 'a' (ă) sound as in the word "bat".

Symbol	Ā, ă
Phonetics	Aye | aa
English	Cake | Bat
French	Gâteau | Chauve-souris
German	Kuchen | Fledermaus
Italian	Torta | Pipistrello
Japanese (Romaji)	Kēki | Kōmori
Korean (RRK)	Keikeu | Bagjwi
Indonesian	Kue | Kelelawar
Mandarin (Hanyu Pinyin)	Dàngāo | Biānfú
Portuguese	Bolo | Morcego
Russian	торт | лапта
Spanish	Pastel | Murciélago

The Letter B

B, b

As a consonant, the letter 'B' does not say its name as do vowels. Rather, it has a short sound as shown below in the phonetic listing. However, there is one case where the "B" sound is silent. This occurs when the letter "b" is combined with the letter "m" at the end of a word in the sequence "mb". In this case, the "m" sound is pronounced but the "b" is silent. An example of this would be the word "lamb".

Phonetics	Buh (very quickly)
English	Bear | Boat | Lamb
French	Ours | Bateau | Agneau
German	Bärin | Boot | Lamm
Italian	Orso | Barca | Agnello
Japanese (Romaji)	Kuma | Bōto | Kohitsuji
Korean (RRK)	Gom | Boteu | Yang-gogi
Indonesian	Beruang | Perahu | Daging domba
Mandarin (Hanyu Pinyin)	Xióng | Chuán | Yángròu
Portuguese	Urso | Barco | Cordeiro
Russian	медведь | лодка | ягненок
Spanish	Oso | Barco | Cordero

The Letter C

C, c

The letter 'C' is unique. It is considered a consonant, but can be used to produce to three distinct sounds. It can have a "Kuh" sound as in "cat", sound similar to the letter "K". It can have an "Sss" sound as in "cycle", similar to the letter "S". And, on some occasions, it is silent when used with another consonant such as the letter "H", producing a "chuh" sound as in the word "church". However, there is always the exception where the letters "ch" together can have a "Kuh" sound, as in the word "chasm".

Phonetics	Kuh (very quickly) | Sss | Chuh (very quickly) | Kuh (very quickly)
English	Cat | Bicycle | Church | Chasm
French	Chat | Vélo | Église | Gouffre
German	Katze | Fahrrad | Kirche | Abgrund
Italian	Gatto | Biciletta | Chiesa | Abisso
Japanese (Romaji)	Neko | Jitensha | Kyōkai | Wareme
Korean (RRK)	Goyang-I | Jajeongeo | Gyohoee | Danjeol
Indonesian	Kucing | Sepeda | Gereja | Jurang
Mandarin (Hanyu Pinyin)	Māo | Zìxíngchē | Jiàohuì | Lièkǒu
Portuguese	Gato | Bicileta | Igreja | Abismo
Russian	Кот | велосипед | церковь | пропасть
Spanish	Gato | Bicicleta | Iglesia | Abismo

The Letter D

D, d

As a consonant, the letter 'D' does not say its name as do vowels. Rather, it has a short sound as shown below in the phonetic listing.

Phonetics	Duh (very quickly)
English	Dog | Duck
French	Chien | Canard
German	Hund | Ente
Italian	Cane | Anatra
Japanese (Romaji)	Inu | Kamo
Korean (RRK)	Gae | Oli
Indonesian	Anjing | Bebek
Mandarin (Hanyu Pinyin)	Gǒu | Yā
Portuguese	Cachorro | Pato
Russian	собака | Утка
Spanish	Perro | Pato

The Letter E
Ē, ĕ

As a vowel, the letter 'E' can appear and sound differently. It can have a long 'E' (Ē) sound as in the word "Eagle", or a short 'e' (ĕ) sound as in the word "Jet".

Symbol	Ē, ĕ
Phonetics	Eee | eh
English	Eagle | Jet
French	Aigle | Jet
German	Adler | Düsenflugzeug
Italian	Aquila | Getto
Japanese (Romaji)	Īguru | Jetto
Korean (RRK)	Dogsuli | Jeteugi
Indonesian	Burung elang | Jet
Mandarin (Hanyu Pinyin)	Yīng | Pēnshè
Portuguese	águia | Jato
Russian	орел | реактивный
Spanish	el águila | Jet

The Letter F

F, f

As a consonant, the letter 'F' does not say its name as do vowels. Rather, it has a short sound as shown below in the phonetic listing.

Phonetics	Fuh (very quickly)
English	Fox | Fish
French	Renard | Pescado
German	Fuchs | Fisch
Italian	Volpe | Pesce
Japanese (Romaji)	Kitsune | Fisshu
Korean (RRK)	Yeou | Mulgogi
Indonesian	Rubah Ikan
Mandarin (Hanyu Pinyin)	Húlí | Diàoyú
Portuguese	Raposa | Peixe
Russian	лиса | Рыба
Spanish	Zorro | Pescado

The Letter G

G, g

The letter 'G' is unique. It is considered a consonant, but can be used to produce to three distinct sounds. It can have a "Guh" sound as in "goat". It can have a "Juh" sound, similar to the letter "J", as in "germ". And, on some occasions, it is silent when used with another consonant such as the letter "N", such as the word "gnosis" (pronounced "noh-sis"), which is taken from the Greek language meaning *knowledge of spiritual matters.*

Phonetics	Guh (very quickly) | Juh (very quickly)
English	Goat | Gorilla | Germ | Gnosis
French	Chèvre | Gorilla | Germ | Gnose
German	Ziege | Gorilla | Keim | Gnosis
Italian	Capra | Gorilla | Germe | Gnosi
Japanese (Romaji)	Yagi | Gorira | Haiga | Reichi
Korean (RRK)	Yeomso | Golilla | Segyun | Geunosiseu
Indonesian	Kambing | Gorila | Kuman | Gnosis
Mandarin (Hanyu Pinyin)	Shānyáng | Dà xīngxīng | Bìngjùn | Zhíjué
Portuguese	Cabra | Gorila | Germe | Gnosis
Russian	козел | горилла | зародыш | гностицизм
Spanish	Cabra | Gorila | Germen | Gnosis

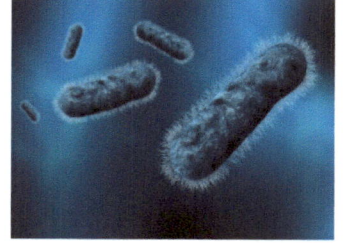

The Letter H

H, h

As a consonant, the letter 'H' does not say its name as do vowels. Rather, it has a short sound as shown below in the phonetic listing.

Phonetics	Huh (very quickly)
English	House | Hammer
French	Maison | Marteau
German	Haus | Hammer
Italian	Casa | Martello
Japanese (Romaji)	Le | Hanmā
Korean (RRK)	Jib | Manchi
Indonesian	Rumah | Palu
Mandarin (Hanyu Pinyin)	Fángzi | Chuí
Portuguese	Casa | Martelo
Russian	дом | молоток
Spanish	Casa | Martillo

The Letter I
Ī, ĭ

As a vowel, the letter 'I' can appear and sound differently. It can have a long 'I' (Ī) sound as in the word "Ice" or a short 'i' (ĭ) sound as in the word "pig". The sound also appears when the letter "I" does not even appear in the word, such as in the word "eye". Finally, on some occasions, it is silent when used with another vowel such as the letter "E", as the word "chief".

Symbol	Ī, ĭ
Phonetics	Eye | ii
English	Ice | Pig | Eye | Chief
French	Glace | Cochon | Oeil | Chef
German	Ice | Schwein | Augen | Häuptling
Italian	Ghiaccio | Maiale | Occhio | Capo
Japanese (Romaji)	Aisu | Buta | Me | Chīfu
Korean (RRK)	Eol-eum | Dwauji | Nun | Dumog
Indonesian	Es | Babi | Mata | Kepala
Mandarin (Hanyu Pinyin)	Bīng | Zhū | Jīng | Shǒuxí
Portuguese	Gelo | Porco | Olho | Chefe
Russian	лед | свинья | око | начальник
Spanish	Helado | Cerdo | Ojo | Jefe

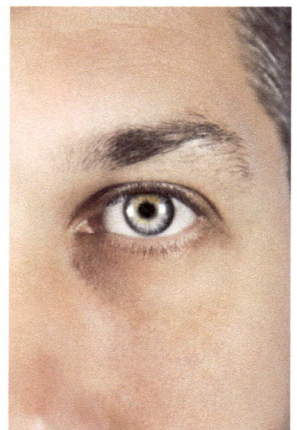

The Letter J

J, j

As a consonant, the letter 'J' does not say its name as do vowels. Rather, it has a short sound as shown below in the phonetic listing.

Phonetics	Juh (very quickly)
English	Jet | Jewel
French	Jet | Bijou
German	Düsenflugzeug | Schmuckstück
Italian	Getto | Gioiello
Japanese (Romaji)	Jetto | Jueru
Korean (RRK)	Jeteugi | Boseog
Indonesian	Jet | Permata
Mandarin (Hanyu Pinyin)	Pēnshè | Bǎoshí
Portuguese	Jato | Jóia
Russian	реактивный | драгоценность
Spanish	Jet | Joya

The Letter K

K, k

As a consonant, the letter 'K' is unique. First, it does not say its name as do vowels. Rather, it has a short sound as shown below in the phonetic listing. Second, on some occasions, it is silent when used with another consonant such as the letter "N", as the word "knife".

Phonetics	Kuh (very quickly)
English	Keg | Kangaroo | Knife
French	Tonnelet | Kangourou | Couteau
German	Keg | Känguru | Messer
Italian	Bariletto | Canguro | Coltello
Japanese (Romaji)	Kegu | Kangarū | Naifu
Korean (RRK)	Jag-eun tong | Kaeng-geolu | Kal
Indonesian	Tong | Kanguru | Pisau
Mandarin (Hanyu Pinyin)	Tǒng | Dàishǔ | Dāo
Portuguese	Barril | Canguru | Faca
Russian	бочонок | кенгуру | нож
Spanish	Barrilete | Canguro | Cuchillo

The Letter L

L, l

As a consonant, the letter 'L' does not say its name as do vowels. Rather, it has a short sound as shown below in the phonetic listing.

Phonetics	ull (very quickly)
English	Leaf | Lamb
French	Feuille | Agneau
German	Blatt | Lamm
Italian	Foglia | Agnello
Japanese (Romaji)	Ha | Kohitsuji
Korean (RRK)	Ip | Yang-gogi
Indonesian	Daun | Daging domba
Mandarin (Hanyu Pinyin)	Shùyè | Yángròu
Portuguese	Folha | Cordeiro
Russian	лист | ягненок
Spanish	Rama | Cordero

The Letter M

M, m

As a consonant, the letter 'M' does not say its name as do vowels. Rather, it has a short sound as shown below in the phonetic listing.

Phonetics	Mmm
English	Mouse | Moon
French	Souris | Lune
German	Maus | Mond
Italian	Topo | Luna
Japanese (Romaji)	Mausu | Tsuki
Korean (RRK)	Jwi | Dal
Indonesian	Tikus | Bulan
Mandarin (Hanyu Pinyin)	lăoshŭ | Yuèqiú
Portuguese	Rato | Lua
Russian	мышь | Луна
Spanish	Ratón | Lina

The Letter N

N, n

As a consonant, the letter 'N' does not say its name as do vowels. Rather, it has a short sound as shown below in the phonetic listing.

Phonetics	Nnn
English	Nail | Nose
French	Clouer | Nez
German	Nagel | Nase
Italian	Chiodo | Naso
Japanese (Romaji)	Neiru | Hana
Korean (RRK)	Mos | Ko
Indonesian	Paku | Hidung
Mandarin (Hanyu Pinyin)	Dīng | Bizi
Portuguese	Prego | Nariz
Russian	гвоздь | нос
Spanish	Clavo | Nariz

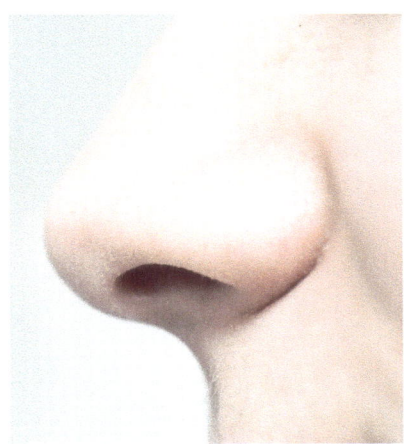

The Letter O
Ō, ŏ

As a vowel, the letter 'O' is unique and can appear and sound differently. It can have a long 'O' (Ō) sound as in the word "Ocean", or a short 'o' (ŏ) sound as in the word "Mop". When combined with another vowel, (either 'oo' or 'oe'), the sound changes again to reflect the vowel with which it was combined.

Symbol	Ō, ŏ
Phonetics	O | Ahh | ooo
English	Ocean | Mop | Shoe
French	Océan | Balai | Chaussure
German	Ozean | Mopp | Schuh
Italian	Oceano | Scopa | Scarpa
Japanese (Romaji)	Kaiyō | Moppu | Kutsu
Korean (RRK)	Daeyang | Cheongso | Gudu
Indonesian	Samudra | Kain pel | Sepatu
Mandarin (Hanyu Pinyin)	Hǎiyáng | Tuōbǎ | Xié
Portuguese	Oceano | Esfregão | Sapato
Russian	океан | швабра | обувной
Spanish	Océano | Trapeador | Zapato

The Letter P

P, p

As a consonant, the letter 'P' is unique. First, it does not say its name as do vowels. Rather, it has a short sound as shown below in the phonetic listing. On some occasions, when it is combined with the letter 'H', it has the same sound as an 'F', as in 'photo'. Finally, when it is combined with letter 'S', the 'P' is silent, as in the word "psalm".

Phonetics	Puh (very quickly) | Fff
English	Pear | Potato | Photo | Psalm
French	Poire | Pomme de terre | Photo | Psaume
German	Birne | Kartoffel | Foto | Psalm
Italian	Pera | Patata | Foto | Salmo
Japanese (Romaji)	Nashi | Poteto | Foto | Shihen
Korean (RRK)	Bae | Gamja | Sajin | Chansong-ga
Indonesian	Pir | Kentang | Foto | Mazmur
Mandarin (Hanyu Pinyin)	Lí | Tǔdòu | Zhàopiàn | Shīpiān
Portuguese	Pera | Batata | Foto | Salmo
Russian	груша | картофель | Фото | Псалом
Spanish	Pera | Patata | Foto | Salmo

The Letter Q

Q, q

As a consonant, the letter 'Q' does not say its name as do vowels. In addition, in the English language, the letter "Q" almost always appears with the vowel letter 'U'. As a result, the two letters together provide a 'koo' sound, as in the word "Quilt".

Phonetics	Koo
English	Quilt
French	Courtepoints
German	Steppdecke
Italian	Trapunta
Japanese (Romaji)	Kiruto
Korean (RRK)	Ibul
Indonesian	Selimut kapas
Mandarin (Hanyu Pinyin)	bèitào
Portuguese	Colcha
Russian	простегивать
Spanish	edredón

The Letter R

R, r

As a consonant, the letter 'R' does not say its name as do vowels. Rather, it has a short sound as shown below in the phonetic listing.

Phonetics	Rrr
English	Rabbit | Rose
French	Lapin | Rose
German	Kaninchen | Rose
Italian	Coniglio | Rosa
Japanese (Romaji)	Usagi | Rōzu
Korean (RRK)	Tokki | Jangmi
Indonesian	Kelinci | Mawar
Mandarin (Hanyu Pinyin)	Tùzǐ | Méiguī
Portuguese	Coelho | Rosa
Russian	кролик | Роза
Spanish	Conejo | Rosa

The Letter S

S, s

As a consonant, the letter 'S' does not say its name as do vowels. Rather, it has a short sound as shown below in the phonetic listing.

Phonetics	Ssss
English	Safe | Store
French	Coffre-fort | Botique
German	Geldschrank | Geschäft
Italian	Cassaforte | Negozio
Japanese (Romaji)	Kinko | Tenpo
Korean (RRK)	Geumgo | Gage
Indonesian	Lemari besi | Toko
Mandarin (Hanyu Pinyin)	Bǎoxiǎnxiāng | Shāngdiàn
Portuguese	Cofre | Loja
Russian	сейф | магазин
Spanish	Caja fuerte | Tienda

The Letter T

T, t

As a consonant, the letter 'T' does not say its name as do vowels. Rather, it has a short sound as shown below in the phonetic listing.

Phonetics	Tuh (very quickly)
English	Tree | Train
French	Arbre | Train
German	Baum | Zug
Italian	Albero | Treno
Japanese (Romaji)	Tsurī | Ressha
Korean (RRK)	Namu | Gicha
Indonesian	Pohon | Kereta api
Mandarin (Hanyu Pinyin)	Shù | Huǒchē
Portuguese	Arvore | Trem
Russian	дерево | поезд
Spanish	Árbol | Tren

The Letter U

Ū, ŭ

As a vowel, the letter 'U' can appear and sound differently. It can have a long 'U' (Ū) sound as in the word "Uniform", or a short 'u' sound (ŭ) as in the word "Bug".

Symbol	Ū, ŭ
Phonetics	You | Uhh
English	Uniform | Bug
French	Uniforme | Punaise
German	Uniform | Käfer
Italian	Divisa | Insetto
Japanese (Romaji)	Seifuku | Bagu
Korean (RRK)	Jebog | Beogeu
Indonesian	Pakaian seragam | Hama
Mandarin (Hanyu Pinyin)	Zhìfú | Chóng
Portuguese	Uniforme | Bicho
Russian	униформа | ошибка
Spanish	Uniforme | Bicho

The Letter V

V, v

As a consonant, the letter 'V' does not say its name as do vowels. Rather, it has a short sound as shown below in the phonetic listing.

Phonetics	Vuh (very quickly)
English	Vase | Violin
French	Vase | Violon
German	Vase | Violine
Italian	Vaso | Violino
Japanese (Romaji)	Kabin | Vu~aiorin
Korean (RRK)	Kkochbyeong | Baiollin
Indonesian	Vas | Biola
Mandarin (Hanyu Pinyin)	Huāpíng | Xiǎotíqín
Portuguese	Vaso | Violino
Russian	ваза | скрипка
Spanish	Florero | Violín

The Letter W

W, w

The letter 'W' is unique. While it is considered a consonant, it can also be used as a vowel. Some linguists, however, say it is more correct to refer to 'W' as a "semi vowel" or "vowel modifier".

Its typical phonetic sound is shown below. However, there are some cases where the "W" sound is silent; that is, it is used in such a way where it appears in a word but has no representative sound. An example of this would be the word "Whole".

Phonetics	Wuh (very quickly)
English	Wagon | Watch
French	Wagon | Montre
German	Wagen | Armbanduhr
Italian	Carro | Orologio
Japanese (Romaji)	Wagon | Udedokei
Korean (RRK)	Sule | Sonmog sigye
Indonesian	Gerobak | Jaga
Mandarin (Hanyu Pinyin)	Chēpí | Shǒubiāo
Portuguese	Vagão | Relógio de pulso
Russian	повозка | часы
Spanish	Vagón | Reloj

The Letter X

X, x

The letter 'X' is considered a consonant and has two unique sounds. Its typical phonetic sound is shown below. However, there are some cases where the "X" sound is silent; that is, it is used in such a way where it appears in a word but has no representative sound. An example of this would be the word "Xylophone".

Phonetics	Echs | KS | Zzz
English	Exit | Six | Xylophone
French	Sortie | Six | Xylophone
German	Ausgang | Sechs | Xylophon
Italian	Uscita | Sei | Xilofono
Japanese (Romaji)	Deguchi | Roku | Mokkin
Korean (RRK)	Chulgu | Yeoseos | Moggeum
Indonesian	Keluar | Enam | Gambang
Mandarin (Hanyu Pinyin)	Chūkǒu | Liù | Mùqín
Portuguese	Saída | Seis | Xilofone
Russian	Выход | шесть | ксилофон
Spanish	Salida | Seis | Xilófono

The Letter Y

Y, y

The letter 'Y' is unique. While it is considered a consonant, it can also be used as a vowel. Some linguists, however, say it is more correct to refer to 'Y' as a "semi vowel" or "vowel modifier".

As shown below, it can have three distinct sounds depending upon its usage. First, are those words in which the letter 'Y' has an 'Eye' sound as in the word "Eye". Second, are those words in which the letter 'Y' has an 'Eee' sound, as in the word "Candy". In these first two instances, the letter 'Y' is considered a vowel. Lastly, are those words in which the letter 'Y' has it a 'Yuh' sound, as in the word "Yoke". In these circumstances, the letter 'Y' is considered a consonant.

Phonetics	Eye | Eee | Yuh (very quickly)
English	Cry | Candy | Yoke
French	Pleueryr | Bonbons | Joug
German	Weinen | Bonbon | Joch
Italian	Piangere | Caramella | Giogo
Japanese (Romaji)	Sakebi | Kyandi | Yōku
Korean (RRK)	Ulda | Satang | Meong-e
Indonesian	Menangis | Permen | Kuk
Mandarin (Hanyu Pinyin)	Kū | Tángguǒ | Joʊk
Portuguese	Chora | Doce | Jugo
Russian	крик | конфеты | ярмо
Spanish	Lloro | Caramelo | Yugo

The Letter Z

Z, z

As a consonant, the letter 'Z' does not say its name as do vowels. Rather, it has a short sound as shown below in the phonetic listing.

Phonetics	Zzz
English	Zebra
French	Zèbre
German	Zebra
Italian	Zebra
Japanese (Romaji)	Shimauma
Korean (RRK)	Eollugmal
Indonesian	Kuda Zebra
Mandarin (Hanyu Pinyin)	Bānmǎ
Portuguese	Zebra
Russian	зебра
Spanish	Zebra

Author's Note

I would like to personally thank you for allowing me the opportunity to share this instructional material with you and your family. As your child begins their life journey into the world of literature, much of their future success will be determined by the level of appreciation they attain in the world of words.

Since we have become a global society, future generations that develop an appreciation for other languages will find more economic and personal satisfaction in life for having taken the time to develop this skill.

As parents, you can take pride in knowing that you are taking a positive first step in guiding the success of your child through developing an appreciation for what other cultures have to offer in a world made smaller by technology, travel, and words.

Best of luck in your journey!

Sincerely,

Brian P. Sheets

Author

Publisher's Note

We would also like to join the author in thanking you for the purchase of Volume 1 in our series Languages of the World and express our appreciation for your taking the time to provide a book review on Amazon.

To obtain 8" x 10" full-color, soft copy versions of this series, please go to the following Amazon links:

Volume 1 – Letters
https://www.amazon.com/dp/B01N9BQMVV

Volume 2 – Numbers
https://www.amazon.com/dp/B01N9C18SG

Volume 3 – Words
https://www.amazon.com/dp/B0787HMNTV

For Academic & Child Care Institutions:

If you would like information on bulk purchases of books in this series *Languages of the World,* please contact the publisher using the information below. Please provide information about your organization and the quantity you are interested in for a price quote.

Customer Service – Institution Sales

Priati Publishing

info@priatipub.com

Other Books by Author

Like this book?

If you like this author's work, your favorable review would be greatly appreciated.

Other publications by this author can be found at:

http://www.priatipub.com

Languages of the World – A Multi-Lingual Introduction to Letters from Around the Globe – Volume 1 **[2017 eLit Gold Award for Education / Academics / Teaching]**

Languages of the World – A Multi-Lingual Introduction to Numbers from Around the Globe – Volume 2 **[2017 eLit Gold Award for Children's Books (7 & Under)]**

Languages of the World – A Multi-Lingual Introduction to Words from Around the Globe – Volume 3

Languages of the World – A Multi-Lingual Introduction to First Sentences from Around the Globe – Volume 4 due out in 2018

The Rest Areas of Your Life   (Kindle eBook)

A Practical Approach to Parenting   (Kindle eBook)

Two Images of God – Discontent   (Suspense Novel)

Endnotes

[1] RRK – Revised Romanization of Korean; released to the public on July 7, 2000 by South Korea's Ministry of Culture and Tourism in Proclamation No. 2000-8.
[2] https://en.wikipedia.org/wiki/Romanization_of_Arabic